And God Spoke

A MESSAGE GOD SPOKE TO ME.
A STUDY OF HIS HEART AND WILL FOR YOUR LIFE.

VOLUME I

DIANE ROSSI

WESTBOW
PRESS®
A DIVISION OF THOMAS NELSON
& ZONDERVAN

WestBow Press books may be ordered through booksellers or by contacting:

WestBow Press
A Division of Thomas Nelson & Zondervan
1663 Liberty Drive
Bloomington, IN 47403
www.westbowpress.com
844-714-3454

Scripture quotations taken from The Holy Bible, New International Version® NIV® Copyright © 1973 1978 1984 2011 by Biblica, Inc. TM. Used by permission. All rights reserved worldwide.

ISBN: 978-1-6642-5757-3 (sc)
ISBN: 978-1-6642-5756-6 (e)

Library of Congress Control Number: 2022902725

Print information available on the last page.

WestBow Press rev. date: 12/07/2022

"In the beginning was
the Word, and the Word
was with God, and
the Word was God."

–John 1:1

Introduction

He chose this space in time for you to occupy for the purpose of being in a relationship with Him and those He created.

He chose to create you. The God of everything *chose* you. Let that sink in for a moment. He wanted you and created you for His purposes, the greatest of which was to be in a relationship with Him—God Almighty. Wow.

He did not create you to be idle and watch life go by. He wants to be part of your life and walk through it with you. He cannot do this unless you have a two-way relationship with Him.

He wants to shower you with His love and to have you experience Him in ways you never have before. Again, this is *God* we are talking about here. He created the world, the universe, beyond what we can imagine. He created light and dark, He created all living things, and He created man and woman. He created everything.

He wants to unleash His Spirit in your life and over the world. He wants you to be a part of that unleashing. He wants to provide a covering for you and give you the rest that you need.

If you seek after Him with your whole heart, He will give you everything that you need. He will give you understanding and insight. He will give you the desire to press into Him to learn everything about Him. You will want to pray and not look at it as a chore or a checkbox. Prayed—check. Read my Bible—check. Did a kind deed—check. No, it will not be a checklist but a desire. A desire to serve Him with everything you have—your heart, mind, spirit, emotions, resources, and so on.

You will not be complacent about your relationship with God anymore but desire to be in prayer, His Word, and fellowship, trying to learn as much as you can.

You will want all that God has for you and seek for the Holy Spirit to guide and direct your life. You will learn to rest in Him and rely on Him for everything.

You will learn not to listen to the lies of the enemy or want to be under the teaching of anyone who is not teaching the truth about God's Word. You will want to be set apart from the world as you grow in your closeness to God.

You may go through stages of repentance, healing, deliverance, restoration, renewal, and ultimately revival. You will desire that others do the same as you experience this new revelation of God and how awesome and powerful He is.

There will be no more excuses for not being in a complete relationship with God. The more you focus on Him, the more the things of this world will seem trivial.

Opposition. God will fight your battles and give you a battleplan for those difficult situations in your life. "For our struggle is not against flesh and blood, but against the rulers, against the authorities, against the powers of this dark world and against the spiritual forces of evil in the heavenly realms" (Ephesians 6:12).

You will understand the sacrifice He made for you with the birth and death of his Son, that you might have eternal life.

You will help others to find their freedom in Christ.

You will know that God's Word is true, infallible, alive, and working in your life as you allow Him to fulfill His promises.

You will know that you are loved beyond a shadow of a doubt—unconditionally.

Your faith will increase as you believe what you learn.

You will understand that God is the beginning and the end—infinite and almighty.

You will leave your desires for worldly things aside and desire only to serve Him and others. As you open yourself to let God work through you, you will want to share what you have learned with others to help them find their completeness in Christ.

And God Spoke

On the day I received the messages contained in this study, I was not feeling well and decided not to attend church. As I crawled into bed, I strongly felt the presence of God. Grabbing a notebook from my nightstand, I started to write what I was hearing, page after page. I was writing so fast that I could barely read what I was writing. It was not until I went back and read each entry that I saw the messages God had for His people. One of these messages was to "feed My sheep." I knew that these messages needed to be shared with His followers. This study is the result of that experience. I pray that you will experience and feel God's presence as deeply as I did that day as you let His words sink into your spirit.

Learning God's Heart and Will for Your Life

Through this study, you will learn about God's heart and will for your life. You will find your purpose. You will bask in the unfathomable and unconditional love that God has for you. You will know why you are here and where you are going—to a place where there is no more crying or pain, a place of absolute peace.

Devote yourself to doing this study as it was designed, following the guidelines, and your life will never be the same. Your focus and prayer life will change to align with God's purposes for you and for those you are in relationships with. You will become excited to see what God will do in and through you as you dedicate yourself to learning His heart and His will.

God wants you to take what you learn and not only apply it to your life but to share it with others. This study can be used individually and for group study. How exciting to share with one another what you will learn about God's character and desires for your life. We need to encourage one another in our walks with Christ. We need to be in unity with Him and others.

How to Use This Study

It is recommended that you have a Bible, a good concordance or internet connection for searching for scriptures, an additional notebook, and a pad of large sticky notes or index cards while you do this study.

This is a self-guided study with the intention of *you* learning what God wants to teach *you* from His Word. As you progress through the study, you may come across words or phrases that are similar to ones you have already explored. Use this as an opportunity to dig even deeper into what God wants you to learn. This is not a study to rush through. In fact, each message should be thoroughly analyzed before moving on to the next one.

Before each study, earnestly pray and ask God for guidance, revelation, insight, and clarity of mind. Pray that He will reveal to you what He wants you to learn from the message. Remove environmental and mental distractions. You will want uninterrupted, unencumbered time with God to be able to hear what He will say to you. Ask God to remove any hindrances in your life that would keep you from hearing His voice and truth.

Open the book to the message you are working on. Read it. Then make it into a prayer that is personal to you. For example, for the fourth message, "Believe in Me, trust in Me, and watch what I, only I, can do," the prayer could be, "Father God, I believe in You. I trust in You. I will be watching for what You and only You can do."

Write this message on a sticky note or index card. You may want more than one. Put them on your car dash, your bathroom mirror, your refrigerator, or anywhere you are likely to see it during the day. Each time you see it, pray the personal prayer and ask God to show you how to apply this to your life.

On the pages after the message, fill out the responses to each of the questions or statements. If you find the space limiting, use a notebook for additional space.

Opening Prayer

Father God,

I come before You now and repent. I repent of anything I have done that has put distance between You and me. I repent of the times You prompted me to move forward and I did not. I repent of those things that I have been involved in that put a division in our relationship.

Forgive me for the times I have put You in a box and have not allowed You the freedom to move. Forgive me for boxing You in by my limited knowledge. Forgive me for the times I have not followed or believed Your Word completely. Remove from me anything that would hinder my relationship with You.

God, open my heart and mind to receive Your message. I pray that You speak to me personally through each message You have provided. Please give me Your insight and wisdom. Use Your Holy Spirit to bring wisdom and teach me. Give me a teachable spirit. Amen.

Be My hands, My voice, My feet.

—And God spoke

Date:_____ Theme of message: _____

My personal prayer for today's message is:

_____
_____
_____
_____
_____

How does this message apply to me?

_____
_____
_____
_____
_____

▷ Search the Bible for scriptures applicable to the message. Write them in your notebook. Be sure to include the scripture reference.

What has God spoken to you through this message?

_____
_____
_____
_____
_____

How can you use this message to show God's unconditional love to others?

_____
_____
_____
_____
_____

▷ Write any notes or additional thoughts in your notebook.

I will give you everything you need.

—And God spoke

Date:_____ Theme of message: _____

My personal prayer for today's message is:

_____
_____
_____
_____
_____

How does this message apply to me?

_____
_____
_____
_____
_____

▷ Search the Bible for scriptures applicable to the message. Write them in your notebook. Be sure to include the scripture reference.

What has God spoken to you through this message?

_____
_____
_____
_____
_____

How can you use this message to show God's unconditional love to others?

_____
_____
_____
_____
_____

▷ Write any notes or additional thoughts in your notebook.

Do not be afraid; I am with you.

—And God spoke

Date:_____ Theme of message: _____

My personal prayer for today's message is:

_____

_____

_____

_____

_____

_____

How does this message apply to me?

_____

_____

_____

_____

_____

▷ Search the Bible for scriptures applicable to the message. Write them in your notebook. Be sure to include the scripture reference.

What has God spoken to you through this message?

_____

_____

_____

_____

_____

How can you use this message to show God's unconditional love to others?

_____

_____

_____

_____

_____

_____

▷ Write any notes or additional thoughts in your notebook.

Believe in Me, trust in Me, and watch what I, only I, can do.

—And God spoke

Date:_____ Theme of message: _____

My personal prayer for today's message is:

_____
_____
_____
_____
_____

How does this message apply to me?

_____
_____
_____
_____
_____

▷ Search the Bible for scriptures applicable to the message. Write them in your notebook.
   Be sure to include the scripture reference.

What has God spoken to you through this message?

_____
_____
_____
_____
_____

How can you use this message to show God's unconditional love to others?

_____
_____
_____
_____
_____

▷ Write any notes or additional thoughts in your notebook.

I did not call My church to be divided but unified.

—And God spoke

Date:_____ Theme of message: _____

My personal prayer for today's message is:

_____
_____
_____
_____
_____

How does this message apply to me?

_____
_____
_____
_____
_____

▷ Search the Bible for scriptures applicable to the message. Write them in your notebook. Be sure to include the scripture reference.

What has God spoken to you through this message?

_____
_____
_____
_____
_____

How can you use this message to show God's unconditional love to others?

_____
_____
_____
_____
_____

▷ Write any notes or additional thoughts in your notebook.

As you unite, good things will happen. The enemy will be stopped.

—And God spoke

Date:_____ Theme of message: _____

My personal prayer for today's message is:

_____

_____

_____

_____

_____

How does this message apply to me?

_____

_____

_____

_____

_____

▷ Search the Bible for scriptures applicable to the message. Write them in your notebook. Be sure to include the scripture reference.

What has God spoken to you through this message?

_____

_____

_____

_____

_____

How can you use this message to show God's unconditional love to others?

_____

_____

_____

_____

_____

▷ Write any notes or additional thoughts in your notebook.

My agenda, My plans, and My Spirit will go forth.

—And God spoke

Date:_____ Theme of message: _____

My personal prayer for today's message is:

_____
_____
_____
_____
_____

How does this message apply to me?

_____
_____
_____
_____
_____

▷ Search the Bible for scriptures applicable to the message. Write them in your notebook. Be sure to include the scripture reference.

What has God spoken to you through this message?

_____
_____
_____
_____
_____

How can you use this message to show God's unconditional love to others?

_____
_____
_____
_____
_____

▷ Write any notes or additional thoughts in your notebook.

The end is near—get ready. Get ready for what I am going to do.

—And God spoke

Date:_____ Theme of message: _____

My personal prayer for today's message is:

_____
_____
_____
_____
_____

How does this message apply to me?

_____
_____
_____
_____
_____

▷ Search the Bible for scriptures applicable to the message. Write them in your notebook. Be sure to include the scripture reference.

What has God spoken to you through this message?

_____
_____
_____
_____
_____

How can you use this message to show God's unconditional love to others?

_____
_____
_____
_____
_____

▷ Write any notes or additional thoughts in your notebook.

I will do things that have never been seen before. I will open eyes to see My glory.

—And God spoke

Date:_____ Theme of message: _____

My personal prayer for today's message is:

_____

_____

_____

_____

_____

How does this message apply to me?

_____

_____

_____

_____

_____

▷ Search the Bible for scriptures applicable to the message. Write them in your notebook. Be sure to include the scripture reference.

What has God spoken to you through this message?

_____

_____

_____

_____

_____

How can you use this message to show God's unconditional love to others?

_____

_____

_____

_____

_____

▷ Write any notes or additional thoughts in your notebook.

You cannot fathom the love I have for My people.

—And God spoke

Date:_____ Theme of message: _____

My personal prayer for today's message is:

_____

_____

_____

_____

_____

How does this message apply to me?

_____

_____

_____

_____

_____

▷ Search the Bible for scriptures applicable to the message. Write them in your notebook. Be sure to include the scripture reference.

What has God spoken to you through this message?

_____

_____

_____

_____

_____

How can you use this message to show God's unconditional love to others?

_____

_____

_____

_____

_____

_____

▷ Write any notes or additional thoughts in your notebook.

Come to Me. I will give you rest.

—And God spoke

Date:_____ Theme of message: _____

My personal prayer for today's message is:

_____

_____

_____

_____

_____

How does this message apply to me?

_____

_____

_____

_____

_____

▷ Search the Bible for scriptures applicable to the message. Write them in your notebook. Be sure to include the scripture reference.

What has God spoken to you through this message?

_____

_____

_____

_____

_____

How can you use this message to show God's unconditional love to others?

_____

_____

_____

_____

_____

▷ Write any notes or additional thoughts in your notebook.

Gather unto Me. I am calling you.

—And God spoke

Date:_____ Theme of message: _____

My personal prayer for today's message is:

_____
_____
_____
_____
_____

How does this message apply to me?

_____
_____
_____
_____
_____

▷ Search the Bible for scriptures applicable to the message. Write them in your notebook. Be sure to include the scripture reference.

What has God spoken to you through this message?

_____
_____
_____
_____
_____

How can you use this message to show God's unconditional love to others?

_____
_____
_____
_____
_____

▷ Write any notes or additional thoughts in your notebook.

I need all of you; remove your doubts and trust in Me.

—And God spoke

Date:_____ Theme of message: _____

My personal prayer for today's message is:

_____
_____
_____
_____
_____

How does this message apply to me?

_____
_____
_____
_____
_____

▷ Search the Bible for scriptures applicable to the message. Write them in your notebook. Be sure to include the scripture reference.

What has God spoken to you through this message?

_____
_____
_____
_____
_____

How can you use this message to show God's unconditional love to others?

_____
_____
_____
_____
_____

▷ Write any notes or additional thoughts in your notebook.

I will fill up the coffers.

—And God spoke

Date:_____ Theme of message: _____

My personal prayer for today's message is:

_____
_____
_____
_____
_____

How does this message apply to me?

_____
_____
_____
_____
_____

▷ Search the Bible for scriptures applicable to the message. Write them in your notebook. Be sure to include the scripture reference.

What has God spoken to you through this message?

_____
_____
_____
_____
_____

How can you use this message to show God's unconditional love to others?

_____
_____
_____
_____
_____

▷ Write any notes or additional thoughts in your notebook.

I knew you before this world and have planned for this moment.

—And God spoke

Date:_____ Theme of message: _____

My personal prayer for today's message is:

_____
_____
_____
_____
_____

How does this message apply to me?

_____
_____
_____
_____
_____

▷ Search the Bible for scriptures applicable to the message. Write them in your notebook. Be sure to include the scripture reference.

What has God spoken to you through this message?

_____
_____
_____
_____
_____

How can you use this message to show God's unconditional love to others?

_____
_____
_____
_____
_____

▷ Write any notes or additional thoughts in your notebook.

Bring Me into the storehouse.

—And God spoke

Date:_____ Theme of message: _____

My personal prayer for today's message is:

_____
_____
_____
_____
_____

How does this message apply to me?

_____
_____
_____
_____
_____

▷ Search the Bible for scriptures applicable to the message. Write them in your notebook. Be sure to include the scripture reference.

What has God spoken to you through this message?

_____
_____
_____
_____
_____

How can you use this message to show God's unconditional love to others?

_____
_____
_____
_____
_____

▷ Write any notes or additional thoughts in your notebook.

You need only Me.

—And God spoke

Date:_____ Theme of message: _____

My personal prayer for today's message is:

_____
_____
_____
_____
_____

How does this message apply to me?

_____
_____
_____
_____
_____

▷ Search the Bible for scriptures applicable to the message. Write them in your notebook. Be sure to include the scripture reference.

What has God spoken to you through this message?

_____
_____
_____
_____
_____

How can you use this message to show God's unconditional love to others?

_____
_____
_____
_____
_____

▷ Write any notes or additional thoughts in your notebook.

Love the unlovely.

—And God spoke

Date:_____ Theme of message: _____

My personal prayer for today's message is:

_____
_____
_____
_____
_____

How does this message apply to me?

_____
_____
_____
_____
_____

▷ Search the Bible for scriptures applicable to the message. Write them in your notebook. Be sure to include the scripture reference.

What has God spoken to you through this message?

_____
_____
_____
_____

How can you use this message to show God's unconditional love to others?

_____
_____
_____
_____
_____

▷ Write any notes or additional thoughts in your notebook.

I will give you the
desires of your heart.

—And God spoke

Date:_____ Theme of message: _____

My personal prayer for today's message is:

_____

_____

_____

_____

_____

How does this message apply to me?

_____

_____

_____

_____

_____

▷ Search the Bible for scriptures applicable to the message. Write them in your notebook. Be sure to include the scripture reference.

What has God spoken to you through this message?

_____

_____

_____

_____

_____

How can you use this message to show God's unconditional love to others?

_____

_____

_____

_____

_____

▷ Write any notes or additional thoughts in your notebook.

Be My heart, My mouth, My word.

—And God spoke

Date:_____ Theme of message: _____

My personal prayer for today's message is:

_____
_____
_____
_____
_____

How does this message apply to me?

_____
_____
_____
_____
_____

▷ Search the Bible for scriptures applicable to the message. Write them in your notebook. Be sure to include the scripture reference.

What has God spoken to you through this message?

_____
_____
_____
_____
_____

How can you use this message to show God's unconditional love to others?

_____
_____
_____
_____
_____

▷ Write any notes or additional thoughts in your notebook.

No more time for complacency.

—And God spoke

Date:_____ Theme of message: _____

My personal prayer for today's message is:

_____
_____
_____
_____
_____

How does this message apply to me?

_____
_____
_____
_____
_____

▷ Search the Bible for scriptures applicable to the message. Write them in your notebook. Be sure to include the scripture reference.

What has God spoken to you through this message?

_____
_____
_____
_____
_____

How can you use this message to show God's unconditional love to others?

_____
_____
_____
_____
_____

▷ Write any notes or additional thoughts in your notebook.

Open the boxes.
Set Me free.

—And God spoke

Date:_____ Theme of message: _____

My personal prayer for today's message is:

_____
_____
_____
_____
_____

How does this message apply to me?

_____
_____
_____
_____
_____

▷ Search the Bible for scriptures applicable to the message. Write them in your notebook. Be sure to include the scripture reference.

What has God spoken to you through this message?

_____
_____
_____
_____
_____

How can you use this message to show God's unconditional love to others?

_____
_____
_____
_____
_____

▷ Write any notes or additional thoughts in your notebook.

Humble yourselves.

—And God spoke

Date:_____ Theme of message: _____

My personal prayer for today's message is:

_____

_____

_____

_____

_____

How does this message apply to me?

_____

_____

_____

_____

_____

▷ Search the Bible for scriptures applicable to the message. Write them in your notebook. Be sure to include the scripture reference.

What has God spoken to you through this message?

_____

_____

_____

_____

_____

How can you use this message to show God's unconditional love to others?

_____

_____

_____

_____

_____

▷ Write any notes or additional thoughts in your notebook.

Unity.

—And God spoke

Date:_____ Theme of message: _____

My personal prayer for today's message is:

_____
_____
_____
_____
_____

How does this message apply to me?

_____
_____
_____
_____
_____

▷ Search the Bible for scriptures applicable to the message. Write them in your notebook. Be sure to include the scripture reference.

What has God spoken to you through this message?

_____
_____
_____
_____
_____

How can you use this message to show God's unconditional love to others?

_____
_____
_____
_____
_____

▷ Write any notes or additional thoughts in your notebook.

Deliverance, healing, restoration.

—And God spoke

Date:_____ Theme of message: _____

My personal prayer for today's message is:

_____

_____

_____

_____

_____

How does this message apply to me?

_____

_____

_____

_____

_____

▷ Search the Bible for scriptures applicable to the message. Write them in your notebook. Be sure to include the scripture reference.

What has God spoken to you through this message?

_____

_____

_____

_____

_____

How can you use this message to show God's unconditional love to others?

_____

_____

_____

_____

_____

▷ Write any notes or additional thoughts in your notebook.

Set the Spirit free.

—And God spoke

Date:_____ Theme of message: _____

My personal prayer for today's message is:

_____

_____

_____

_____

_____

How does this message apply to me?

_____

_____

_____

_____

_____

▷ Search the Bible for scriptures applicable to the message. Write them in your notebook. Be sure to include the scripture reference.

What has God spoken to you through this message?

_____

_____

_____

_____

_____

How can you use this message to show God's unconditional love to others?

_____

_____

_____

_____

_____

▷ Write any notes or additional thoughts in your notebook.

Intercessory
prayer groups.

—And God spoke

Date:_____ Theme of message: _____

My personal prayer for today's message is:

_____
_____
_____
_____
_____

How does this message apply to me?

_____
_____
_____
_____
_____

▷ Search the Bible for scriptures applicable to the message. Write them in your notebook. Be sure to include the scripture reference.

What has God spoken to you through this message?

_____
_____
_____
_____
_____

How can you use this message to show God's unconditional love to others?

_____
_____
_____
_____
_____

▷ Write any notes or additional thoughts in your notebook.

Not about man's mandate but Mine.

—And God spoke

Date:_____ Theme of message: _____

My personal prayer for today's message is:

_____
_____
_____
_____
_____

How does this message apply to me?

_____
_____
_____
_____
_____

▷ Search the Bible for scriptures applicable to the message. Write them in your notebook. Be sure to include the scripture reference.

What has God spoken to you through this message?

_____
_____
_____
_____
_____

How can you use this message to show God's unconditional love to others?

_____
_____
_____
_____
_____

▷ Write any notes or additional thoughts in your notebook.

The time is now!
Don't hold Me back.

—And God spoke

Date:_____ Theme of message: _____

My personal prayer for today's message is:

_____
_____
_____
_____
_____

How does this message apply to me?

_____
_____
_____
_____
_____

▷ Search the Bible for scriptures applicable to the message. Write them in your notebook. Be sure to include the scripture reference.

What has God spoken to you through this message?

_____
_____
_____
_____
_____

How can you use this message to show God's unconditional love to others?

_____
_____
_____
_____
_____

▷ Write any notes or additional thoughts in your notebook.

Cry out for Me—
all of Me.

—And God spoke

Date:_____ Theme of message: _____

My personal prayer for today's message is:

_____

_____

_____

_____

_____

How does this message apply to me?

_____

_____

_____

_____

_____

▷ Search the Bible for scriptures applicable to the message. Write them in your notebook. Be sure to include the scripture reference.

What has God spoken to you through this message?

_____

_____

_____

_____

_____

How can you use this message to show God's unconditional love to others?

_____

_____

_____

_____

_____

▷ Write any notes or additional thoughts in your notebook.

My Spirit is anxious to move.

—And God spoke

Date:_____ Theme of message: _____

My personal prayer for today's message is:

_____
_____
_____
_____
_____

How does this message apply to me?

_____
_____
_____
_____
_____

▷ Search the Bible for scriptures applicable to the message. Write them in your notebook. Be sure to include the scripture reference.

What has God spoken to you through this message?

_____
_____
_____
_____
_____

How can you use this message to show God's unconditional love to others?

_____
_____
_____
_____
_____

▷ Write any notes or additional thoughts in your notebook.

Remove the weights.

—And God spoke

Date:_____ Theme of message: _____

My personal prayer for today's message is:

_____
_____
_____
_____
_____

How does this message apply to me?

_____
_____
_____
_____
_____

▷ Search the Bible for scriptures applicable to the message. Write them in your notebook. Be sure to include the scripture reference.

What has God spoken to you through this message?

_____
_____
_____
_____
_____

How can you use this message to show God's unconditional love to others?

_____
_____
_____
_____
_____

▷ Write any notes or additional thoughts in your notebook.

Your focus is not on the right things.

—And God spoke

Date:_____ Theme of message: _____

My personal prayer for today's message is:

_____
_____
_____
_____
_____

How does this message apply to me?

_____
_____
_____
_____
_____

▷ Search the Bible for scriptures applicable to the message. Write them in your notebook. Be sure to include the scripture reference.

What has God spoken to you through this message?

_____
_____
_____
_____
_____

How can you use this message to show God's unconditional love to others?

_____
_____
_____
_____
_____

▷ Write any notes or additional thoughts in your notebook.

You are too concerned about the things of this world.

—And God spoke

Date:_____ Theme of message: _____

My personal prayer for today's message is:

_____
_____
_____
_____
_____

How does this message apply to me?

_____
_____
_____
_____
_____

▷ Search the Bible for scriptures applicable to the message. Write them in your notebook. Be sure to include the scripture reference.

What has God spoken to you through this message?

_____
_____
_____
_____
_____

How can you use this message to show God's unconditional love to others?

_____
_____
_____
_____
_____

▷ Write any notes or additional thoughts in your notebook.

I am not of this
world, and soon you
will not be either.

—And God spoke

Date:_____ Theme of message: _____

My personal prayer for today's message is:

_____
_____
_____
_____
_____

How does this message apply to me?

_____
_____
_____
_____
_____

▷ Search the Bible for scriptures applicable to the message. Write them in your notebook. Be sure to include the scripture reference.

What has God spoken to you through this message?

_____
_____
_____
_____
_____

How can you use this message to show God's unconditional love to others?

_____
_____
_____
_____
_____

▷ Write any notes or additional thoughts in your notebook.

Rely only on Me.

—And God spoke

Date:_____ Theme of message: _____

My personal prayer for today's message is:

_____
_____
_____
_____
_____

How does this message apply to me?

_____
_____
_____
_____
_____

▷ Search the Bible for scriptures applicable to the message. Write them in your notebook. Be sure to include the scripture reference.

What has God spoken to you through this message?

_____
_____
_____
_____
_____

How can you use this message to show God's unconditional love to others?

_____
_____
_____
_____
_____

▷ Write any notes or additional thoughts in your notebook.

I will thwart the enemy. My foot will stomp his head.

—And God spoke

Date:_____ Theme of message: _____

My personal prayer for today's message is:

_____
_____
_____
_____
_____

How does this message apply to me?

_____
_____
_____
_____
_____

▷ Search the Bible for scriptures applicable to the message. Write them in your notebook. Be sure to include the scripture reference.

What has God spoken to you through this message?

_____
_____
_____
_____
_____

How can you use this message to show God's unconditional love to others?

_____
_____
_____
_____
_____

▷ Write any notes or additional thoughts in your notebook.

There will be opposition, but remember I came to overcome the world.

—And God spoke

Date:_____ Theme of message: _____

My personal prayer for today's message is:

_____

_____

_____

_____

_____

How does this message apply to me?

_____

_____

_____

_____

_____

▷ Search the Bible for scriptures applicable to the message. Write them in your notebook. Be sure to include the scripture reference.

What has God spoken to you through this message?

_____

_____

_____

_____

_____

How can you use this message to show God's unconditional love to others?

_____

_____

_____

_____

_____

▷ Write any notes or additional thoughts in your notebook.

You will be overcomers.

—And God spoke

Date:_____ Theme of message: _____

My personal prayer for today's message is:

_____
_____
_____
_____
_____

How does this message apply to me?

_____
_____
_____
_____
_____

▷ Search the Bible for scriptures applicable to the message. Write them in your notebook. Be sure to include the scripture reference.

What has God spoken to you through this message?

_____
_____
_____
_____
_____

How can you use this message to show God's unconditional love to others?

_____
_____
_____
_____
_____

▷ Write any notes or additional thoughts in your notebook.

I sent My Son for a purpose.
That purpose is now—
to set the captive free.

—And God spoke

Date:_____ Theme of message: _____

My personal prayer for today's message is:

_____
_____
_____
_____
_____
_____

How does this message apply to me?

_____
_____
_____
_____
_____

▷ Search the Bible for scriptures applicable to the message. Write them in your notebook. Be sure to include the scripture reference.

What has God spoken to you through this message?

_____
_____
_____
_____
_____

How can you use this message to show God's unconditional love to others?

_____
_____
_____
_____
_____
_____

▷ Write any notes or additional thoughts in your notebook.

Bring them together in unity.

—And God spoke

Date:_____ Theme of message: _____

My personal prayer for today's message is:

_____

_____

_____

_____

_____

How does this message apply to me?

_____

_____

_____

_____

_____

▷ Search the Bible for scriptures applicable to the message. Write them in your notebook. Be sure to include the scripture reference.

What has God spoken to you through this message?

_____

_____

_____

_____

_____

How can you use this message to show God's unconditional love to others?

_____

_____

_____

_____

_____

▷ Write any notes or additional thoughts in your notebook.

I will use the young and the old.

—And God spoke

Date:_____ Theme of message: _____

My personal prayer for today's message is:

_____
_____
_____
_____
_____

How does this message apply to me?

_____
_____
_____
_____
_____

▷ Search the Bible for scriptures applicable to the message. Write them in your notebook. Be sure to include the scripture reference.

What has God spoken to you through this message?

_____
_____
_____
_____
_____

How can you use this message to show God's unconditional love to others?

_____
_____
_____
_____
_____

▷ Write any notes or additional thoughts in your notebook.

I want those who want Me and put Me first in all things.

—And God spoke

Date:_____ Theme of message: _____

My personal prayer for today's message is:

_____
_____
_____
_____
_____

How does this message apply to me?

_____
_____
_____
_____
_____

▷ Search the Bible for scriptures applicable to the message. Write them in your notebook. Be sure to include the scripture reference.

What has God spoken to you through this message?

_____
_____
_____
_____
_____

How can you use this message to show God's unconditional love to others?

_____
_____
_____
_____
_____

▷ Write any notes or additional thoughts in your notebook.

I am the Alpha and the Omega.

—And God spoke

Date:_____ Theme of message: _____

My personal prayer for today's message is:

_____

_____

_____

_____

_____

How does this message apply to me?

_____

_____

_____

_____

_____

▷ Search the Bible for scriptures applicable to the message. Write them in your notebook. Be sure to include the scripture reference.

What has God spoken to you through this message?

_____

_____

_____

_____

_____

How can you use this message to show God's unconditional love to others?

_____

_____

_____

_____

_____

▷ Write any notes or additional thoughts in your notebook.

There is no one who can come before Me or after Me.

—And God spoke

Date:_____ Theme of message: _____

My personal prayer for today's message is:

_____
_____
_____
_____
_____

How does this message apply to me?

_____
_____
_____
_____
_____

▷ Search the Bible for scriptures applicable to the message. Write them in your notebook. Be sure to include the scripture reference.

What has God spoken to you through this message?

_____
_____
_____
_____
_____

How can you use this message to show God's unconditional love to others?

_____
_____
_____
_____
_____

▷ Write any notes or additional thoughts in your notebook.

I am that I am.

—And God spoke

Date:_____ Theme of message: _____

My personal prayer for today's message is:

_____
_____
_____
_____
_____

How does this message apply to me?

_____
_____
_____
_____
_____

▷ Search the Bible for scriptures applicable to the message. Write them in your notebook. Be sure to include the scripture reference.

What has God spoken to you through this message?

_____
_____
_____
_____
_____

How can you use this message to show God's unconditional love to others?

_____
_____
_____
_____
_____

▷ Write any notes or additional thoughts in your notebook.

Take up your cross
and follow Me.

—And God spoke

Date:_____ Theme of message: _____

My personal prayer for today's message is:

_____

_____

_____

_____

_____

How does this message apply to me?

_____

_____

_____

_____

_____

▷ Search the Bible for scriptures applicable to the message. Write them in your notebook. Be sure to include the scripture reference.

What has God spoken to you through this message?

_____

_____

_____

_____

_____

How can you use this message to show God's unconditional love to others?

_____

_____

_____

_____

_____

▷ Write any notes or additional thoughts in your notebook.

My burden is light, but
My heart is heavy to
set the captives free.

—And God spoke

Date:_____ Theme of message: _____

My personal prayer for today's message is:

_____⌇

_____

_____

_____

_____

_____

How does this message apply to me?

_____⌇

_____

_____

_____

_____

_____

▷ Search the Bible for scriptures applicable to the message. Write them in your notebook. Be sure to include the scripture reference.

What has God spoken to you through this message?

_____⌇

_____

_____

_____

_____

_____

How can you use this message to show God's unconditional love to others?

_____⌇

_____

_____

_____

_____

_____

_____

▷ Write any notes or additional thoughts in your notebook.

The wolf will bare
his teeth, but I will
shut his mouth.

—And God spoke

Date:_____ Theme of message: _____

My personal prayer for today's message is:

_____
_____
_____
_____
_____
_____

How does this message apply to me?

_____
_____
_____
_____
_____
_____

▷ Search the Bible for scriptures applicable to the message. Write them in your notebook. Be sure to include the scripture reference.

What has God spoken to you through this message?

_____
_____
_____
_____
_____

How can you use this message to show God's unconditional love to others?

_____
_____
_____
_____
_____
_____

▷ Write any notes or additional thoughts in your notebook.

Nothing will be able to stop what I have planned.

—And God spoke

Date:_____ Theme of message: _____

My personal prayer for today's message is:

_____
_____
_____
_____
_____

How does this message apply to me?

_____
_____
_____
_____
_____

▷ Search the Bible for scriptures applicable to the message. Write them in your notebook. Be sure to include the scripture reference.

What has God spoken to you through this message?

_____
_____
_____
_____
_____

How can you use this message to show God's unconditional love to others?

_____
_____
_____
_____
_____

▷ Write any notes or additional thoughts in your notebook.

Stay close to Me.

—And God spoke

Date:_____ Theme of message: _____

My personal prayer for today's message is:

_____
_____
_____
_____
_____

How does this message apply to me?

_____
_____
_____
_____
_____

▷ Search the Bible for scriptures applicable to the message. Write them in your notebook. Be sure to include the scripture reference.

What has God spoken to you through this message?

_____
_____
_____
_____
_____

How can you use this message to show God's unconditional love to others?

_____
_____
_____
_____
_____
_____

▷ Write any notes or additional thoughts in your notebook.

Worship Me.

—And God spoke

Date:_____ Theme of message: _____

My personal prayer for today's message is:

_____
_____
_____
_____
_____

How does this message apply to me?

_____
_____
_____
_____
_____

▷ Search the Bible for scriptures applicable to the message. Write them in your notebook. Be sure to include the scripture reference.

What has God spoken to you through this message?

_____
_____
_____
_____
_____

How can you use this message to show God's unconditional love to others?

_____
_____
_____
_____
_____

▷ Write any notes or additional thoughts in your notebook.

Seek Me.

—And God spoke

Date:_____ Theme of message: _____

My personal prayer for today's message is:

_____
_____
_____
_____
_____

How does this message apply to me?

_____
_____
_____
_____
_____

▷ Search the Bible for scriptures applicable to the message. Write them in your notebook. Be sure to include the scripture reference.

What has God spoken to you through this message?

_____
_____
_____
_____
_____

How can you use this message to show God's unconditional love to others?

_____
_____
_____
_____
_____

▷ Write any notes or additional thoughts in your notebook.

Want all of Me as I want all of you.

—And God spoke

Date:_____ Theme of message: _____

My personal prayer for today's message is:

_____
_____
_____
_____
_____

How does this message apply to me?

_____
_____
_____
_____
_____

▷ Search the Bible for scriptures applicable to the message. Write them in your notebook. Be sure to include the scripture reference.

What has God spoken to you through this message?

_____
_____
_____
_____
_____

How can you use this message to show God's unconditional love to others?

_____
_____
_____
_____
_____
_____

▷ Write any notes or additional thoughts in your notebook.

You are My child.

—And God spoke

Date:_____ Theme of message: _____

My personal prayer for today's message is:

_____
_____
_____
_____
_____

How does this message apply to me?

_____
_____
_____
_____
_____

▷ Search the Bible for scriptures applicable to the message. Write them in your notebook. Be sure to include the scripture reference.

What has God spoken to you through this message?

_____
_____
_____
_____
_____

How can you use this message to show God's unconditional love to others?

_____
_____
_____
_____
_____

▷ Write any notes or additional thoughts in your notebook.

I love you. Never forget that.

—And God spoke

Date:_____ Theme of message: _____

My personal prayer for today's message is:

_____
_____
_____
_____
_____

How does this message apply to me?

_____
_____
_____
_____
_____

▷ Search the Bible for scriptures applicable to the message. Write them in your notebook. Be sure to include the scripture reference.

What has God spoken to you through this message?

_____
_____
_____
_____
_____

How can you use this message to show God's unconditional love to others?

_____
_____
_____
_____
_____

▷ Write any notes or additional thoughts in your notebook.

I will not leave or abandon you.

—And God spoke

Date:_____ Theme of message: _____

My personal prayer for today's message is:

_____
_____
_____
_____
_____

How does this message apply to me?

_____
_____
_____
_____
_____

▷ Search the Bible for scriptures applicable to the message. Write them in your notebook. Be sure to include the scripture reference.

What has God spoken to you through this message?

_____
_____
_____
_____
_____

How can you use this message to show God's unconditional love to others?

_____
_____
_____
_____
_____

▷ Write any notes or additional thoughts in your notebook.

Believe.

—And God spoke

Date:_____ Theme of message: _____

My personal prayer for today's message is:

_____
_____
_____
_____
_____

How does this message apply to me?

_____
_____
_____
_____
_____

▷ Search the Bible for scriptures applicable to the message. Write them in your notebook. Be sure to include the scripture reference.

What has God spoken to you through this message?

_____
_____
_____
_____
_____

How can you use this message to show God's unconditional love to others?

_____
_____
_____
_____
_____

▷ Write any notes or additional thoughts in your notebook.

I will put back things that have been torn apart.

—And God spoke

Date:_____ Theme of message: _____

My personal prayer for today's message is:

_____

_____

_____

_____

_____

How does this message apply to me?

_____

_____

_____

_____

_____

▷ Search the Bible for scriptures applicable to the message. Write them in your notebook.
    Be sure to include the scripture reference.

What has God spoken to you through this message?

_____

_____

_____

_____

_____

How can you use this message to show God's unconditional love to others?

_____

_____

_____

_____

_____

▷ Write any notes or additional thoughts in your notebook.

My veil will be unveiled.

—And God spoke

Date:_____ Theme of message: _____

My personal prayer for today's message is:

_____
_____
_____
_____
_____

How does this message apply to me?

_____
_____
_____
_____
_____

▷ Search the Bible for scriptures applicable to the message. Write them in your notebook. Be sure to include the scripture reference.

What has God spoken to you through this message?

_____
_____
_____
_____
_____

How can you use this message to show God's unconditional love to others?

_____
_____
_____
_____
_____

▷ Write any notes or additional thoughts in your notebook.

I have sewn together a great veil of covering for My people. Stay under My veil.

—And God spoke

Date:_____ Theme of message: _____

My personal prayer for today's message is:

_____
_____
_____
_____
_____

How does this message apply to me?

_____
_____
_____
_____
_____

▷ Search the Bible for scriptures applicable to the message. Write them in your notebook. Be sure to include the scripture reference.

What has God spoken to you through this message?

_____
_____
_____
_____
_____

How can you use this message to show God's unconditional love to others?

_____
_____
_____
_____
_____

▷ Write any notes or additional thoughts in your notebook.

Do not look to your left nor your right.

—And God spoke

Date:_____ Theme of message: _____

My personal prayer for today's message is:

_____
_____
_____
_____
_____

How does this message apply to me?

_____
_____
_____
_____
_____

▷ Search the Bible for scriptures applicable to the message. Write them in your notebook. Be sure to include the scripture reference.

What has God spoken to you through this message?

_____
_____
_____
_____
_____

How can you use this message to show God's unconditional love to others?

_____
_____
_____
_____
_____

▷ Write any notes or additional thoughts in your notebook.

Keep your focus on Me.

—And God spoke

Date:_____ Theme of message: _____

My personal prayer for today's message is:

_____
_____
_____
_____
_____

How does this message apply to me?

_____
_____
_____
_____
_____

▷ Search the Bible for scriptures applicable to the message. Write them in your notebook. Be sure to include the scripture reference.

What has God spoken to you through this message?

_____
_____
_____
_____
_____

How can you use this message to show God's unconditional love to others?

_____
_____
_____
_____
_____

▷ Write any notes or additional thoughts in your notebook.

I am the Almighty, the Everlasting, the Beginning, and the End.

—And God spoke

Date:_____ Theme of message: _____

My personal prayer for today's message is:

_____
_____
_____
_____
_____

How does this message apply to me?

_____
_____
_____
_____
_____

▷ Search the Bible for scriptures applicable to the message. Write them in your notebook. Be sure to include the scripture reference.

What has God spoken to you through this message?

_____
_____
_____
_____
_____

How can you use this message to show God's unconditional love to others?

_____
_____
_____
_____
_____

▷ Write any notes or additional thoughts in your notebook.

I will find and give favor to those who seek Me.

—And God spoke

Date:_____ Theme of message: _____

My personal prayer for today's message is:

_____

_____

_____

_____

_____

How does this message apply to me?

_____

_____

_____

_____

_____

▷ Search the Bible for scriptures applicable to the message. Write them in your notebook. Be sure to include the scripture reference.

What has God spoken to you through this message?

_____

_____

_____

_____

_____

How can you use this message to show God's unconditional love to others?

_____

_____

_____

_____

_____

_____

▷ Write any notes or additional thoughts in your notebook.

I will not be stopped.

—And God spoke

Date:_____ Theme of message: _____

My personal prayer for today's message is:

_____
_____
_____
_____
_____

How does this message apply to me?

_____
_____
_____
_____
_____

▷ Search the Bible for scriptures applicable to the message. Write them in your notebook. Be sure to include the scripture reference.

What has God spoken to you through this message?

_____
_____
_____
_____
_____

How can you use this message to show God's unconditional love to others?

_____
_____
_____
_____
_____

▷ Write any notes or additional thoughts in your notebook.

Put aside your foolish behavior and cling to Me.

—And God spoke

Date:_____ Theme of message: _____

My personal prayer for today's message is:

_____
_____
_____
_____
_____

How does this message apply to me?

_____
_____
_____
_____
_____

▷ Search the Bible for scriptures applicable to the message. Write them in your notebook. Be sure to include the scripture reference.

What has God spoken to you through this message?

_____
_____
_____
_____
_____

How can you use this message to show God's unconditional love to others?

_____
_____
_____
_____
_____

▷ Write any notes or additional thoughts in your notebook.

I can be your only answer.

—And God spoke

Date:_____ Theme of message: _____

My personal prayer for today's message is:

_____
_____
_____
_____
_____

How does this message apply to me?

_____
_____
_____
_____
_____

▷ Search the Bible for scriptures applicable to the message. Write them in your notebook. Be sure to include the scripture reference.

What has God spoken to you through this message?

_____
_____
_____
_____
_____

How can you use this message to show God's unconditional love to others?

_____
_____
_____
_____
_____

▷ Write any notes or additional thoughts in your notebook.

Yes, I made this world; but you are not of it.

—And God spoke

Date:_____ Theme of message: _____

My personal prayer for today's message is:

_____

_____

_____

_____

_____

How does this message apply to me?

_____

_____

_____

_____

_____

▷ Search the Bible for scriptures applicable to the message. Write them in your notebook. Be sure to include the scripture reference.

What has God spoken to you through this message?

_____

_____

_____

_____

_____

How can you use this message to show God's unconditional love to others?

_____

_____

_____

_____

_____

_____

▷ Write any notes or additional thoughts in your notebook.

You are Mine.

—And God spoke

Date:_____ Theme of message: _____

My personal prayer for today's message is:

_____
_____
_____
_____
_____

How does this message apply to me?

_____
_____
_____
_____
_____

▷ Search the Bible for scriptures applicable to the message. Write them in your notebook. Be sure to include the scripture reference.

What has God spoken to you through this message?

_____
_____
_____
_____
_____

How can you use this message to show God's unconditional love to others?

_____
_____
_____
_____
_____

▷ Write any notes or additional thoughts in your notebook.

Rest in Me.

—And God spoke

Date:_____ Theme of message: _____

My personal prayer for today's message is:

_____
_____
_____
_____
_____

How does this message apply to me?

_____
_____
_____
_____
_____

▷ Search the Bible for scriptures applicable to the message. Write them in your notebook. Be sure to include the scripture reference.

What has God spoken to you through this message?

_____
_____
_____
_____
_____

How can you use this message to show God's unconditional love to others?

_____
_____
_____
_____
_____

▷ Write any notes or additional thoughts in your notebook.

Contemplate Me.

—And God spoke

Date:_____ Theme of message: _____

My personal prayer for today's message is:

_____

_____

_____

_____

_____

How does this message apply to me?

_____

_____

_____

_____

_____

▷ Search the Bible for scriptures applicable to the message. Write them in your notebook. Be sure to include the scripture reference.

What has God spoken to you through this message?

_____

_____

_____

_____

_____

How can you use this message to show God's unconditional love to others?

_____

_____

_____

_____

_____

▷ Write any notes or additional thoughts in your notebook.

Cling to Me.

—And God spoke

Date:_____ Theme of message: _____

My personal prayer for today's message is:

_____
_____
_____
_____
_____

How does this message apply to me?

_____
_____
_____
_____
_____

▷ Search the Bible for scriptures applicable to the message. Write them in your notebook. Be sure to include the scripture reference.

What has God spoken to you through this message?

_____
_____
_____
_____
_____

How can you use this message to show God's unconditional love to others?

_____
_____
_____
_____
_____

▷ Write any notes or additional thoughts in your notebook.

Come to Me. I am calling you.

—And God spoke

Date:_____ Theme of message: _____

My personal prayer for today's message is:

_____

_____

_____

_____

_____

How does this message apply to me?

_____

_____

_____

_____

_____

_____

▷ Search the Bible for scriptures applicable to the message. Write them in your notebook. Be sure to include the scripture reference.

What has God spoken to you through this message?

_____

_____

_____

_____

_____

How can you use this message to show God's unconditional love to others?

_____

_____

_____

_____

_____

_____

▷ Write any notes or additional thoughts in your notebook.

Calling you to the nations, to the people.

—And God spoke

Date:_____ Theme of message: _____

My personal prayer for today's message is:

_____
_____
_____
_____
_____

How does this message apply to me?

_____
_____
_____
_____
_____

▷ Search the Bible for scriptures applicable to the message. Write them in your notebook. Be sure to include the scripture reference.

What has God spoken to you through this message?

_____
_____
_____
_____
_____

How can you use this message to show God's unconditional love to others?

_____
_____
_____
_____
_____

▷ Write any notes or additional thoughts in your notebook.

Bring My Word, My
healing, My deliverance,
My Love, My provision,
My help, My security.

—And God spoke

Date:_____ Theme of message: _____

My personal prayer for today's message is:

_____
_____
_____
_____
_____

How does this message apply to me?

_____
_____
_____
_____
_____

▷ Search the Bible for scriptures applicable to the message. Write them in your notebook. Be sure to include the scripture reference.

What has God spoken to you through this message?

_____
_____
_____
_____
_____

How can you use this message to show God's unconditional love to others?

_____
_____
_____
_____
_____

▷ Write any notes or additional thoughts in your notebook.

I will open the storehouses and pour forth My Spirit on the land.

—And God spoke

Date:_____ Theme of message: _____

My personal prayer for today's message is:

_____
_____
_____
_____
_____

How does this message apply to me?

_____
_____
_____
_____
_____

▷ Search the Bible for scriptures applicable to the message. Write them in your notebook. Be sure to include the scripture reference.

What has God spoken to you through this message?

_____
_____
_____
_____
_____

How can you use this message to show God's unconditional love to others?

_____
_____
_____
_____
_____

▷ Write any notes or additional thoughts in your notebook.

Weeping will last but for a moment.

–And God spoke

Date:_____ Theme of message: _____

My personal prayer for today's message is:

_____
_____
_____
_____
_____

How does this message apply to me?

_____
_____
_____
_____
_____

▷ Search the Bible for scriptures applicable to the message. Write them in your notebook. Be sure to include the scripture reference.

What has God spoken to you through this message?

_____
_____
_____
_____
_____

How can you use this message to show God's unconditional love to others?

_____
_____
_____
_____
_____

▷ Write any notes or additional thoughts in your notebook.

A new day is coming.

—And God spoke

Date:_____ Theme of message: _____

My personal prayer for today's message is:

_____

_____

_____

_____

_____

How does this message apply to me?

_____

_____

_____

_____

_____

▷ Search the Bible for scriptures applicable to the message. Write them in your notebook. Be sure to include the scripture reference.

What has God spoken to you through this message?

_____

_____

_____

_____

_____

How can you use this message to show God's unconditional love to others?

_____

_____

_____

_____

_____

_____

▷ Write any notes or additional thoughts in your notebook.

A day when I will reign in all My glory and splendor.

—And God spoke

Date:_____ Theme of message: _____

My personal prayer for today's message is:

_____
_____
_____
_____
_____
_____

How does this message apply to me?

_____
_____
_____
_____
_____

▷ Search the Bible for scriptures applicable to the message. Write them in your notebook. Be sure to include the scripture reference.

What has God spoken to you through this message?

_____
_____
_____
_____
_____

How can you use this message to show God's unconditional love to others?

_____
_____
_____
_____
_____
_____

▷ Write any notes or additional thoughts in your notebook.

Won't you come with Me?

—And God spoke

Date:_____ Theme of message: _____

My personal prayer for today's message is:

_____
_____
_____
_____
_____

How does this message apply to me?

_____
_____
_____
_____
_____

▷ Search the Bible for scriptures applicable to the message. Write them in your notebook. Be sure to include the scripture reference.

What has God spoken to you through this message?

_____
_____
_____
_____
_____

How can you use this message to show God's unconditional love to others?

_____
_____
_____
_____
_____

▷ Write any notes or additional thoughts in your notebook.

Put away your childish
things; you are not a
child anymore. You are
My children but not a
child. It is time to grow
up and be My people.

—And God spoke

Date:_____ Theme of message: _____

My personal prayer for today's message is:

_____

_____

_____

_____

_____

How does this message apply to me?

_____

_____

_____

_____

_____

▷ Search the Bible for scriptures applicable to the message. Write them in your notebook. Be sure to include the scripture reference.

What has God spoken to you through this message?

_____

_____

_____

_____

_____

How can you use this message to show God's unconditional love to others?

_____

_____

_____

_____

_____

▷ Write any notes or additional thoughts in your notebook.

Be My people—
committed only to Me.

—And God spoke

Date:_____ Theme of message: _____

My personal prayer for today's message is:

_____

_____

_____

_____

_____

How does this message apply to me?

_____

_____

_____

_____

_____

▷ Search the Bible for scriptures applicable to the message. Write them in your notebook. Be sure to include the scripture reference.

What has God spoken to you through this message?

_____

_____

_____

_____

_____

How can you use this message to show God's unconditional love to others?

_____

_____

_____

_____

_____

▷ Write any notes or additional thoughts in your notebook.

Let Me be your God— your only God.

–And God spoke

Date:_____ Theme of message: _____

My personal prayer for today's message is:

_____
_____
_____
_____
_____

How does this message apply to me?

_____
_____
_____
_____
_____

▷ Search the Bible for scriptures applicable to the message. Write them in your notebook. Be sure to include the scripture reference.

What has God spoken to you through this message?

_____
_____
_____
_____
_____

How can you use this message to show God's unconditional love to others?

_____
_____
_____
_____
_____

▷ Write any notes or additional thoughts in your notebook.

I will not have anything else before Me.

—And God spoke

Date:_____ Theme of message: _____

My personal prayer for today's message is:

_____
_____
_____
_____
_____

How does this message apply to me?

_____
_____
_____
_____
_____

▷ Search the Bible for scriptures applicable to the message. Write them in your notebook. Be sure to include the scripture reference.

What has God spoken to you through this message?

_____
_____
_____
_____
_____

How can you use this message to show God's unconditional love to others?

_____
_____
_____
_____
_____
_____

▷ Write any notes or additional thoughts in your notebook.

Clean your house. Remove those things that you keep from Me.

—And God spoke

Date:_____ Theme of message: _____

My personal prayer for today's message is:

_____
_____
_____
_____
_____
_____

How does this message apply to me?

_____
_____
_____
_____
_____
_____

▷ Search the Bible for scriptures applicable to the message. Write them in your notebook. Be sure to include the scripture reference.

What has God spoken to you through this message?

_____
_____
_____
_____
_____
_____

How can you use this message to show God's unconditional love to others?

_____
_____
_____
_____
_____
_____

▷ Write any notes or additional thoughts in your notebook.

I am to be your number one.

–And God spoke

Date:_____ Theme of message: _____

My personal prayer for today's message is:

_____
_____
_____
_____
_____
_____

How does this message apply to me?

_____
_____
_____
_____
_____
_____

▷ Search the Bible for scriptures applicable to the message. Write them in your notebook. Be sure to include the scripture reference.

What has God spoken to you through this message?

_____
_____
_____
_____
_____
_____

How can you use this message to show God's unconditional love to others?

_____
_____
_____
_____
_____
_____

▷ Write any notes or additional thoughts in your notebook.

I desire all of you.

–And God spoke

Date:_____ Theme of message: _____

My personal prayer for today's message is:

_____
_____
_____
_____
_____

How does this message apply to me?

_____
_____
_____
_____
_____

▷ Search the Bible for scriptures applicable to the message. Write them in your notebook. Be sure to include the scripture reference.

What has God spoken to you through this message?

_____
_____
_____
_____
_____

How can you use this message to show God's unconditional love to others?

_____
_____
_____
_____
_____

▷ Write any notes or additional thoughts in your notebook.

I desire that you want all of Me.

–And God spoke

Date:_____ Theme of message: _____

My personal prayer for today's message is:

_____

_____

_____

_____

_____

How does this message apply to me?

_____

_____

_____

_____

_____

▷ Search the Bible for scriptures applicable to the message. Write them in your notebook. Be sure to include the scripture reference.

What has God spoken to you through this message?

_____

_____

_____

_____

_____

How can you use this message to show God's unconditional love to others?

_____

_____

_____

_____

_____

_____

▷ Write any notes or additional thoughts in your notebook.

Watch what I can do when you give Me your all.

—And God spoke

Date:_____ Theme of message: _____

My personal prayer for today's message is:

_____

_____

_____

_____

_____

How does this message apply to me?

_____

_____

_____

_____

_____

▷ Search the Bible for scriptures applicable to the message. Write them in your notebook. Be sure to include the scripture reference.

What has God spoken to you through this message?

_____

_____

_____

_____

_____

How can you use this message to show God's unconditional love to others?

_____

_____

_____

_____

_____

_____

▷ Write any notes or additional thoughts in your notebook.

You cannot imagine or think of the things I am capable of.

—And God spoke

Date:_____ Theme of message: _____

My personal prayer for today's message is:

_____

_____

_____

_____

_____

How does this message apply to me?

_____

_____

_____

_____

_____

▷ Search the Bible for scriptures applicable to the message. Write them in your notebook. Be sure to include the scripture reference.

What has God spoken to you through this message?

_____

_____

_____

_____

_____

How can you use this message to show God's unconditional love to others?

_____

_____

_____

_____

_____

▷ Write any notes or additional thoughts in your notebook.

Feed My sheep. They are hungry. I am anxious to feed them.

—And God spoke

Date:_____ Theme of message: _____

My personal prayer for today's message is:

_____
_____
_____
_____
_____
_____

How does this message apply to me?

_____
_____
_____
_____
_____

▷ Search the Bible for scriptures applicable to the message. Write them in your notebook. Be sure to include the scripture reference.

What has God spoken to you through this message?

_____
_____
_____
_____
_____
_____

How can you use this message to show God's unconditional love to others?

_____
_____
_____
_____
_____
_____

▷ Write any notes or additional thoughts in your notebook.

I know all, see all. Nothing is hidden from Me.

—And God spoke

Date:_____ Theme of message: _____

My personal prayer for today's message is:

_____
_____
_____
_____
_____

How does this message apply to me?

_____
_____
_____
_____
_____

▷ Search the Bible for scriptures applicable to the message. Write them in your notebook. Be sure to include the scripture reference.

What has God spoken to you through this message?

_____
_____
_____
_____
_____

How can you use this message to show God's unconditional love to others?

_____
_____
_____
_____
_____
_____

▷ Write any notes or additional thoughts in your notebook.

Repent. Repent that I may give you My Spirit and its fullness.

—And God spoke

Date:_____ Theme of message: _____

My personal prayer for today's message is:

_____

_____

_____

_____

_____

_____

How does this message apply to me?

_____

_____

_____

_____

_____

_____

▷ Search the Bible for scriptures applicable to the message. Write them in your notebook. Be sure to include the scripture reference.

What has God spoken to you through this message?

_____

_____

_____

_____

_____

_____

How can you use this message to show God's unconditional love to others?

_____

_____

_____

_____

_____

_____

_____

▷ Write any notes or additional thoughts in your notebook.

Repent that I may use you.

—And God spoke

Date:_____ Theme of message: _____

My personal prayer for today's message is:

_____⤳

_____

_____

_____

_____

_____

How does this message apply to me?

_____⤳

_____

_____

_____

_____

_____

▷ Search the Bible for scriptures applicable to the message. Write them in your notebook. Be sure to include the scripture reference.

What has God spoken to you through this message?

_____⤳

_____

_____

_____

_____

_____

How can you use this message to show God's unconditional love to others?

_____⤳

_____

_____

_____

_____

_____

_____

▷ Write any notes or additional thoughts in your notebook.

Repent that the plans of the enemy might be stopped.

–And God spoke

Date:_____ Theme of message: _____

My personal prayer for today's message is:

_____
_____
_____
_____
_____

How does this message apply to me?

_____
_____
_____
_____
_____

▷ Search the Bible for scriptures applicable to the message. Write them in your notebook. Be sure to include the scripture reference.

What has God spoken to you through this message?

_____
_____
_____
_____
_____

How can you use this message to show God's unconditional love to others?

_____
_____
_____
_____
_____

▷ Write any notes or additional thoughts in your notebook.

I have an abundance to give you—more than you can fathom or imagine.

—And God spoke

Date:_____ Theme of message: _____

My personal prayer for today's message is:

_____
_____
_____
_____
_____

How does this message apply to me?

_____
_____
_____
_____
_____

▷ Search the Bible for scriptures applicable to the message. Write them in your notebook. Be sure to include the scripture reference.

What has God spoken to you through this message?

_____
_____
_____
_____
_____

How can you use this message to show God's unconditional love to others?

_____
_____
_____
_____
_____
_____

▷ Write any notes or additional thoughts in your notebook.

I love My people and want them free. Free to be free in Me.

—And God spoke

Date:_____ Theme of message: _____

My personal prayer for today's message is:

_____

_____

_____

_____

_____

_____

How does this message apply to me?

_____

_____

_____

_____

_____

_____

▷ Search the Bible for scriptures applicable to the message. Write them in your notebook. Be sure to include the scripture reference.

What has God spoken to you through this message?

_____

_____

_____

_____

_____

_____

How can you use this message to show God's unconditional love to others?

_____

_____

_____

_____

_____

_____

▷ Write any notes or additional thoughts in your notebook.

Just keep walking in My ways, and I will direct your path.

—And God spoke

Date:_____ Theme of message: _____

My personal prayer for today's message is:

_____

_____

_____

_____

_____

How does this message apply to me?

_____

_____

_____

_____

_____

▷ Search the Bible for scriptures applicable to the message. Write them in your notebook. Be sure to include the scripture reference.

What has God spoken to you through this message?

_____

_____

_____

_____

_____

How can you use this message to show God's unconditional love to others?

_____

_____

_____

_____

_____

▷ Write any notes or additional thoughts in your notebook.

I will open doors that
man cannot open and
close doors that should
not be opened.

—And God spoke

Date:_____ Theme of message: _____

My personal prayer for today's message is:

_____
_____
_____
_____
_____

How does this message apply to me?

_____
_____
_____
_____
_____

▷ Search the Bible for scriptures applicable to the message. Write them in your notebook. Be sure to include the scripture reference.

What has God spoken to you through this message?

_____
_____
_____
_____
_____

How can you use this message to show God's unconditional love to others?

_____
_____
_____
_____
_____

▷ Write any notes or additional thoughts in your notebook.

Epilogue

By the time you read this, I pray that you have gained a new understanding of God and His purposes for you. To learn more about God and His Holy Spirit, get a copy of the study, *And God Spoke, a Study of God's Will and Heart for Your Life, Volume II.* Below is an excerpt from the book.

How often have you contained God by your beliefs, indoctrinations, or other's interpretations of His Word? God requests that you be completely and unabashedly open to Him and what He desires. He does not want you to limit Him by your preconceived ideas of who He is or what He can accomplish. Rather, He wants you to search His word in its entirety while praying for understanding to learn His true character and how to be positioned in His will.

Do you want to experience a new level of intimacy with God? Then, wholeheartedly put aside your own desires and agendas positioning yourself to be in a complete relationship with Him. You were created to be in communion with God, to offer Him praises, and to share His love with others. That is His will.

God desires to release His Holy Spirit to move in the lives of His people.

God is anxious to move, but He wants our attention and readiness. It is time to open the boxes and set God free.

"And afterward, I will pour out my Spirit on all people. Your sons and daughters will prophesy, your old men will dream dreams, your young men will see visions. Even on my servants, both men and women, I will pour out my Spirit in those days" (Joel 2:28–29).

The scriptures say that we have not because we ask not. What if we appeal to God for a greater move of His Spirit? What if our time was spent seeking God and all that He has to offer?

God put us on this earth to commune with Him and those He created. He wants a relationship with us. He provided His Spirit as one who intercedes on our behalf, as a comforter and as a reminder to help us live lives of faith.

His Spirit is available for everyone. "For we were all baptized by one Spirit so as to form one body—whether Jews or Gentiles, slave or free—and we were all given the one Spirit to drink" (1 Corinthians 12:13). Jesus had Him come into the world to act on our behalf, leading us in truth and knowledge.

"For those who are led by the Spirit of God are the children of God. The Spirit you received does not make you slaves, so that you live in fear again; rather, the Spirit you received brought about your adoption to sonship. And by him we cry, "Abba, Father." The Spirit himself testifies with our spirit that we are God's children" (Romans 8:14–16).

God, I ask that those who do not know You in Your completeness, nor are aware of Your Holy Spirit today, would reach out to You and ask for the infilling of Your Spirit. Thank You that You have provided one to intercede on our behalf, to comfort us and seal us with the testament that we are Your children. Give to each of us the gifts that we need to be able to bring others closer to You. Amen.